Project Elephant

Susan Ring

Weigl Publishers Inc.

Editor
Diana Marshall

Design and Layout
Warren Clark
Bryan Pezzi

Copy Editor
Heather Kissock

Photo Researcher
Tina Schwartzenberger

DEVELOPED IN COLLABORATION WITH THE PITTSBURGH ZOO AND PPG AQUARIUM

Published by Weigl Publishers Inc.
123 South Broad Street, Box 227
Mankato, MN 56002   USA
Web site: www.weigl.com

Library of Congress Cataloging-in-Publication Data

Ring, Susan.
  Project elephantnew / Susan Ring.
    p. cm. -- (Zoo life)
  ISBN 1-59036-016-8 (lib. bdg. : alk. paper)
  1. African elephant--Infancy--Juvenile literature. 2. Zoo animals--Pennsylvania--Pittsburgh--Juvenile literature. [1. African elephant. 2. Elephants. 3. Animals--Infancy. 4. Zoo animals.] I. Title. II. Series. III. Zoo life (Mankato, Minn.)
  QL737.P98 R556 2002
  599.67'139--dc21

                                        2002006396

Printed in the United States of America
1 2 3 4 5 6 7 8 9 0 06 05 04 03 02

Photograph Credits
Every reasonable effort has been made to trace ownership and to obtain permission to reprint copyright material. The publishers would be pleased to have any errors or omissions brought to their attention so that they may be corrected in subsequent printings.

Cover: baby African elephant (Corel Corporation); **CORBIS/MAGMA:** page 20; **Corel Corporation:** pages 11, 17 middle, 17 far right, 19, 22 top, 22 bottom, 23; **Brian Keating:** page 21; **Thomas Kitchin/Tom Stack & Associates:** pages 9, 16; **Bruce Leighty:** title page, page 18; **Joe McDonald/Tom Stack & Associates:** page 17 left; **PhotoDisc, Inc.:** page 17 far left; **Courtesy of the Pittsburgh Zoo and PPG Aquarium:** pages 3, 4, 5, 6, 7, 8, 10, 12, 13, 14, 15, 17 right.

Contents

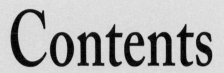

A Baby is Born

After 10 hours of **labor**, a new life began. At about 1 o'clock on a mid-September afternoon, a baby African elephant was born in an **enclosure** at the Pittsburgh Zoo and PPG Aquarium. This healthy male weighed 257 pounds. He was born with dark, curly hair on his head.

Zoo Issues

Should baby zoo animals share enclosures with their mother? Why?

■ The newborn elephant had pink-gray skin. His feet were as white as snow.

It took only 15 minutes for the newborn elephant to stand on his own. He communicated with his mother right away, using different sounds. This helped them form a **bond**. The baby elephant did not **nurse** for the first 2 hours. Instead, he tried out his trunk. He also tried to figure out where his mother's milk was. His mother helped by pulling him to her and positioning him.

A half-hour after he was born, the baby elephant was walking. Despite being curious, he never strayed far from his mother.

Meet the Baby

T he zoo's elephant manager, Willie Theison, chose the newborn elephant's name. He gave the calf a name so he could communicate with him. The zoo does not want his name used in public. The zoo feels it is important to remember that the baby is a wild animal. The baby is an **ambassador** for all the African elephants in the world. He can help the zoo teach people about the importance of animal **conservation**.

■ The new baby is not a pet or a performer. At the zoo, he represents all African elephants.

Zoo Issues

Should newborn baby animals be put on public display?

■ The baby learned how to act with the other elephants by staying close to his mother and watching her responses.

At first, the baby and his mother were kept in an area away from the other elephants. This helped them get to know each other. The calf learned to recognize his mother's appearance, smells, and sounds. After a few days, the mother and baby joined the elephant **herd**. It was important for the baby to understand his role and the role of others in the herd.

Trunk Tricks

Like all baby elephants, the zoo's new baby watched the others in the herd. The other elephants looked out for him. He learned that his mother was the boss. He also learned which of the other elephants he could play with. Using his trunk was one of the first skills he learned. At first, he stepped on it and tripped over it. Sometimes, he would suck on it. It took him a few weeks to learn to control his trunk.

The baby elephant learned new skills from his mother, his aunts, and his cousins.

- Between 6 and 8 months of age, calves begin to control their trunks. They use their trunks to eat and drink.

- Elephants begin to grow tusks at about 2 years of age.

- Sometimes, a herd will take in lost or **orphaned** babies.

By the time he was 5 weeks old, the calf learned to use mud to block the sun and get rid of insects. He rolled around to cover his skin with a layer of dirt. Later, he figured out how to eat and drink with his trunk. This took plenty of practice.

The baby elephant grew quickly. He loved to swim. He spent much time playing in the mud. He was full of energy and very curious. For fun, he enjoyed annoying his sister. His favorite activity was to chase the peacocks around the African elephant **exhibit**. He also loved chewing and playing with hoses.

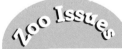

Zoo Issues

Why is it important for zoo food to be similar to animals' food in the wild?

Meet the Parents

The baby elephant's mother was born in Africa in 1982. She was rescued when she was 2 years old. She was an orphan. She came to the Pittsburgh Zoo and PPG Aquarium from a **sanctuary** in Florida. The newborn elephant is her second baby, but her first successful birth. The calf's father, born in 1979, was orphaned at 2 years of age. He came to the zoo in 1994.

Zoo Issues

Should breeding in zoos be controlled and monitored?

■ The baby elephant's mother weighs about 7,000 pounds.

- The African elephant **breeding program** at the Pittsburgh Zoo and PPG Aquarium directs research. It studies how elephants communicate with each other. It also studies their memory, intelligence, and reactions to medicine.

- Young elephants enjoy playing. They run at each other, butt heads, and grab each other's tails. These activities help them learn the social skills needed to survive in the wild.

- Female African elephants are ready to mate at 9 years of age. Male African elephants are ready to mate when they are 11 or 12 years old.

The mother and father were introduced slowly through bars that separated them. This was done so that **zookeepers** could see if the elephants liked each other. The female loved the male right away. For the next 2 days, the two African elephants were put in one enclosure. They spent a few hours each day together. Almost 2 years later, the calf was born.

All in the Family

In the wild, elephant herds consist of related females and their calves. Older males only join the herd to mate. In the zoo, when mating was complete, the calf's father was kept in a separate yard. He could see and touch the mother and baby through the enclosure. He did not help care for the baby.

Zoo Issues

Think of some reasons why zoo animals may need to be separated.

When the baby elephant becomes a teenager, the group will force him to leave. He will be moved to another enclosure.

- The Pittsburgh Zoo and PPG Aquarium feeds the elephants hay, grass, trees, and 20 pounds of fruit and vegetables each day. This is similar to an elephant's diet in the wild.

- The elephants at the Pittsburgh Zoo and PPG Aquarium are fed a peanut butter and Vitamin E sandwich every day.

- In the wild, female elephants spend their lifetime in the herd. Males leave the group when they are 10 to 15 years old. In zoos, males may be forced to leave the herd when they become teenagers.

The Pittsburgh Zoo and PPG Aquarium started a special breeding program to save the shrinking **captive** elephant population. The new calf was the second baby successfully born into the program. The babies will keep the population of captive African elephants stable in North America. As part of the program, female elephants are taught to raise and care for babies. The goal is to teach them to become good mothers.

The Zoo Crew

The African elephant exhibit has a pool for swimming and sand for digging. Elephants roll in a mud hole and play with logs and branches. These features copy the elephants' natural **habitat**. The zoo's **curators** choose plants and trees that are safe for the elephants to eat. The elephants are walked daily to get extra exercise.

■ Elephants like to bathe. A large pool helps the zoo's African elephants stay healthy, happy, and active.

The zoo's elephant manager decides which elephants should be together by monitoring their actions. He also trains the elephants. The **veterinarians** keep the elephants healthy. They give the elephants medicine, **vaccines,** and checkups. Sometimes, they have to pull infected tusks out.

Zookeepers feed and bathe the elephants and clean the exhibit. They get to know each elephant very well.

HOW CAN I BECOME A CURATOR?

A curator finds and obtains new animals. Curators also maintain animal information. To become a curator, an advanced degree is needed. On-the-job training is also required. A love for animals is helpful. Experience can be gained by volunteering at a local zoo.

Animal Gear

African elephants are the largest land animals on Earth. They have many features that cannot be missed. While other animals might have large noses, no other animal has a trunk.

Zoo Issues

Why should zoo enclosures be similar to an animal's natural habitat?

Skin
Elephants' thick skin protects them from thorny bushes and insect bites. In some spots, their skin is up to 3 inches thick. Elephants cool off and protect their skin from burning by rolling in mud and dirt. The deep wrinkles in their skin hold moisture. This helps them keep cool in the sun.

Trunk
An elephant's trunk contains about 150,000 muscles. The trunk acts like a hand, a nose, a trumpet, and a hose. It can pull apart entire trees. It can pluck one tiny berry off a vine. Elephants use their trunks to spray water, scratch, call out, touch, smell, and breathe.

Ears
Elephants have big ears that do more than provide keen hearing. African elephants flap their ears back and forth to stay cool and to communicate with each other. Each elephant has a unique pattern of small holes or tears along the edges of their ears.

Legs and Feet
Elephants walk on their toes, which easily support their huge bodies. A layer of padding between their toes and on the soles of their feet acts like a mattress. It absorbs the elephant's full weight. It also allows elephants to walk quietly.

Teeth
Tusks are very long teeth. They are made of **ivory**. Elephants use their tusks to peel bark off trees and dig for water. Four **molars** grind plants and bark. These teeth become worn, fall out, and grow back 5 or 6 times. One pair of tusks must last a lifetime.

In the Wild

Elephants are very social animals. They always travel in herds. African elephants live on the savanna. A herd consists of related females, such as mothers, sisters, aunts, grandmothers, cousins, and their babies. Except for the older males, who mostly live alone, elephants depend on each other for their survival. Herd members eat, drink, and rest within a few yards of each other. If an elephant falls behind, others in the herd will stop and wait.

An elephant herd can have two to twenty-nine members.

One African elephant can eat between 300 and 600 pounds of food in a day. An elephant can drink between 30 and 50 gallons of water in a day. To find that much food and water, elephants must spend much of their time walking. They can walk 20 to 50 miles in a day. Elephants are herbivores. This means they eat only plants. Elephants must find a great deal of roots, leaves, and grasses to satisfy their hunger.

BRAIN BOOSTERS

- Elephants digest only half of their food. Elephant droppings contain plant seeds and grass that were not digested. These droppings **fertilize** the soil.

- The leader of the herd is usually the oldest and largest female. She is called the matriarch. Matriarchs are 40 to 50 years old.

- Despite their size and loud trumpeting noises, elephants are usually gentle animals. Their screeching, ear flapping, and rumbling are happy greetings to other herd members.

■ Elephants do not use their trunks like straws. Instead, they drink by sucking water into their trunks and then releasing it into their mouths.

Trading Tusks

In the wild, elephants have few enemies because they are so large. Humans are their main enemy. Elephants are hunted for their ivory tusks. Hunting has caused a drop in elephant populations. In 1989, many countries agreed to stop the ivory trade. This has helped. Still, elephants continue to be killed by illegal hunters. **Game reserves** have been set up in parts of Africa to help conserve elephants in the wild.

▧ When an elephant herd travels in search of food and water, its members often walk in single file behind the matriarch.

BRAIN BOOSTERS

- In the wild, African elephants can live to 60 or 70 years of age. In zoos, they often live longer.

- When there is little rain, elephants use their tusks to dig through dirt. They dig until they find water to drink. Other thirsty animals share the water the elephants bring to the surface.

- Today, there are fewer than 500,000 African elephants left in the wild.

Loss of habitat is another threat to African elephants in the wild. As human populations grow, people build on the grasslands that elephants need for food. Trees are cut down and plant life is destroyed to make way for farms, ranches, and cities. Elephants in zoos teach visitors about the importance of balancing human needs with what is best for the conservation of the African elephants.

Zoo Issues

How can zoos help wild animal populations?

Elephant Issues

Benefits of Zoo Life

- No danger from hunting, competition, or habitat loss
- Regular food, play time, and medical care
- Can help educate the public about elephants
- Is easier to research elephants in zoos
- Breeding programs maintain a stable zoo population
- Can live a longer life

Benefits of Life in the Wild

- More natural space in which to feed and live
- Maintain diverse African elephant populations
- Daily mental and physical challenges, such as finding food
- Part of the natural web of life consisting of plants, predators, and prey
- Live complex lives
- Maintain independence

Folk Tale

Extra-strength Elephant

To avoid the hard work of plowing his field, clever Hare challenges big African Elephant and Muddy Hippopotamus to a tug-of-war. The two large beasts laugh at the idea. They are confident in their strength and size. What they do not realize is that each time they pull the rope, they plow another row in Hare's field.

Source: Schatz, Letta. *The Extraordinary Tug-of War*.
New York: Follett Publishing Company, 1968.

More Information

The Internet can lead you to some exciting information on elephants. Try searching on your own, or visit the following Web sites:

American Zoo and Aquarium Association (AZA)
www.aza.org

In the Wild: Africa
www.bagheera.com/inthewild/van_anim_elephant.htm

National Geographic Kids
www.nationalgeographic.com/kids/
creature_feature/0103/elephants.html

Pittsburgh Zoo and PPG Aquarium
www.pittsburghzoo.com

CONSERVATION GROUPS

There are many organizations involved in elephant research and conservation. You can get information on elephants by writing to the following addresses:

INTERNATIONAL
Born Free Foundation/
Elefriends
Cherry Tree Cottage
Coldharbour
Dorking, Surrey, UK
RH5 6HA

UNITED STATES
Amboseli Elephant
Research Project
African Wildlife Foundation
1717 Massachusetts Ave. N.W.
Washington, DC 20036

Words to Know

ambassador: one who represents all others in a group

bond: close relationship

breeding program: producing babies by mating selected animals

captive: kept in an enclosure; not in the wild

conservation: the care and monitoring of animals and animal populations for their continued existence

curators: people who control the kinds and numbers of animals living in a zoo

enclosure: closed-in area that is designed to copy an animal's home in the wild

exhibit: a space on display that looks similar to an animal's natural habitat

fertilize: to put nutrients into the soil to promote plant growth

game reserves: large areas of protected land for wild animals

habitat: place in the wild where an animal naturally lives

herd: group of animals that live and travel together

ivory: hard, white material that makes up an elephant's tusks

labor: giving birth

molars: broad teeth used for grinding

nurse: drink a mother's milk

orphaned: left without parents

sanctuary: a safe place for animals

savanna: wide, open grasslands in Africa

species: a group that shares biological features

vaccines: medicines to prevent sickness

veterinarians: animal doctors

zookeepers: people at a zoo who feed and take care of the animals

Index